Sticker Fashionista

by Kelly Smith

Published in 2012 by Laurence King Publishing Ltd, 361–373 City Road, London EC1V 1LR, United Kingdom
Tel: + 44 20 7841 6900, Fax: + 44 20 7841 6910, e-mail: enquiries@laurenceking.com, www.laurenceking.com

Copyright © illustrations 2012 Kelly Smith
Text and research by Maia-Adams

A catalogue record for this book is available from the British Library.

ISBN: 978 1 78067 017 1

Design: Eleanor Ridsdale
Printed in Malaysia

French Fancies

Haute couture (meaning 'high fashion' in French) has its home in Paris. In special studios called ateliers, fashion houses such as Chanel and Christian Dior create gowns and suits that are made to measure. Because each piece is entirely handmade, couture takes many hours to create and costs a small fortune to buy!

If money were no object, what would be your dream couture creation?

Made in Manhattan

With its famous designer labels like Marc Jacobs, Anna Sui and Calvin Klein, New York is the perfect city to indulge in year-round retail therapy. Hot summers are ideal for sassy separates and bold sunglasses, while crisp winters make killer heels, sharp tailoring and to-die-for coats a must.

Put together an outfit for your favourite season.

BIG IN JAPAN

In certain areas of Tokyo, young fashionistas go to great lengths to express their personal style. Some like bright wigs, quirky bags and girly frills while others prefer to customize their technicolour clothes with pins and cartoonish bows. Some even dress up as giant cuddly toys!

Express yourself with a unique outfit from your Tokyo wardrobe.

Street Life

When it comes to street style, Londoners rule! From glamorous goths rocking all-black wardrobes and skater girls with their sportswear vibe, to the mix-and-match ensembles of with-it bloggers, it's no wonder trend hunters and fashion designers the world over look to London's style tribes for inspiration.

Create an individual look based on the style tribe you'd like to belong to.

ANIMAL INSTINCT

With its ability to make an outfit exotic, no wonder designers like Italian Roberto Cavalli and American Donna Karan turn to animal print again and again. From leopard spots and zebra stripes to snaky scales, whether you wear it head to toe, or just on your boots and bag, animal print lets you take a walk on the wild side.

Pick a print and bring out your inner animal.

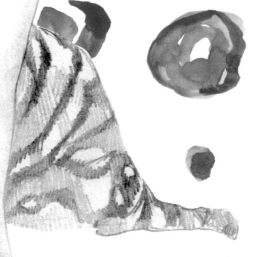

Flower Power

Whether you're dressing up in a beautiful gown, or dressing down in leggings and a tee, a floral print always looks fresh and a corsage enhances any outfit. From abstracted petals and exotic blossoms to dainty buds, not only is the flower print versatile, it's blooming lovely too!

Create a nature-inspired backdrop to complement your flowery look.

The Fab Fifties

1950s fashion was so cute. Full billowing skirts, nipped-in waists, capped sleeves and cropped trousers were flattering and girly. Peep-toe sandals, a sprinkling of bows and a candy store colour palette added the finishing touches to a look that's just as fresh today.

If you and a friend wore 1950s-style clothes, which items would you pick?

French Fancies

Made in
Manhattan

BIG IN
JAPAN

Street
Life

ANIMAL
INSTINCT

FlowerPower

The Fab
Fifties

Catwalk
Queen

CELEBRITY STYLE

HELLO SAILOR

Jeans Genius

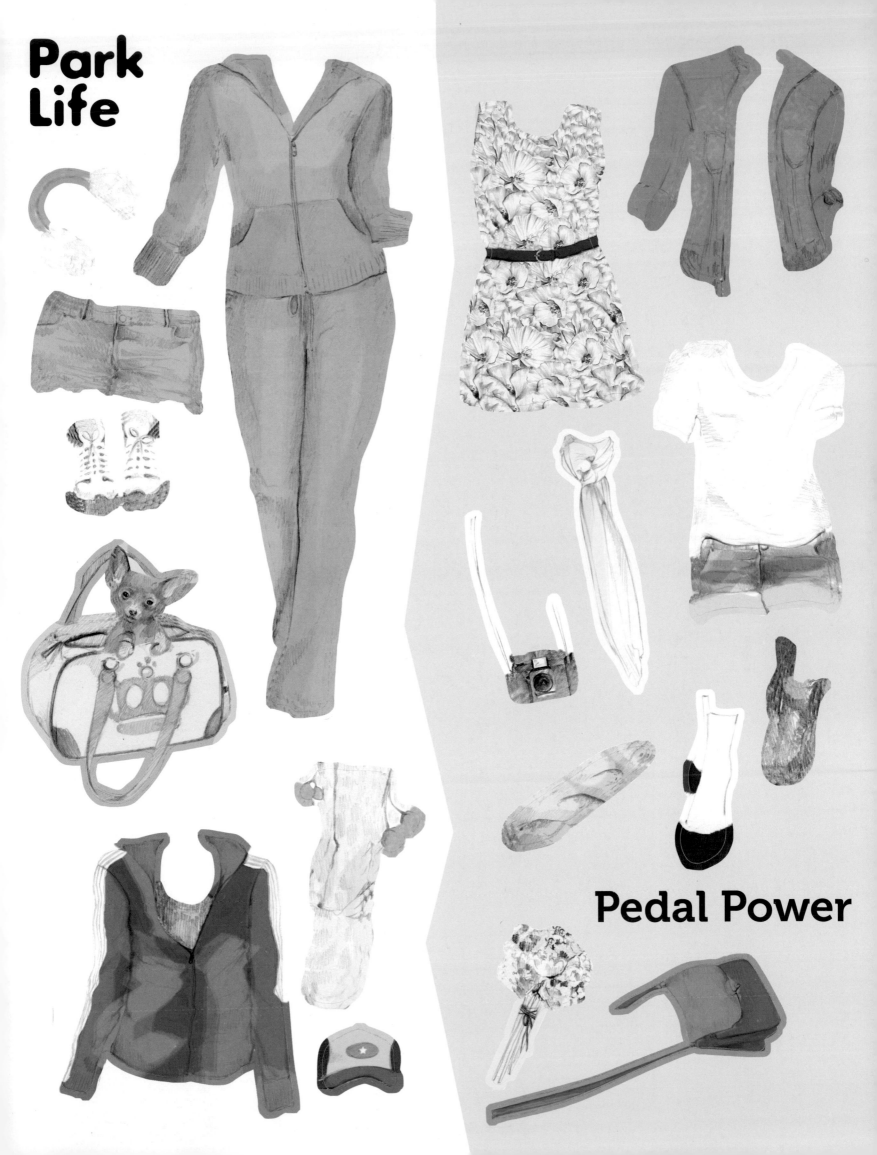

Park Life

Pedal Power

Easy Does It

The
Swinging
Sixties

Hidden Identities

FESTIVAL CHIC

Catwalk Queen

Twice a year the world's top designers get to show off their new collections on catwalks in London, Paris, New York and Milan. Each city is known for a certain kind of style, but for glamour – think figure-hugging dresses, slim-fitting pants and sky-high stilettos by Gucci, Dolce & Gabbana and Fendi – Milan wins hands down.

What's the most glamorous look you can think of?

CELEBRITY STYLE

Red carpet looks take a lot of preparation. Perfect make-up, glossy locks and sparkly jewels are key. But the out-of-this-world gowns are the real star players. Using light-as-a-feather fabrics to create backless, strapless, fabulous confections, designers like Louis Vuitton, Valentino and Balenciaga ensure A-list celebrities look a million dollars when the cameras flash.

It's your moment in the spotlight. Pick a dress that's guaranteed to get you noticed.

Jeans Genius

Denim is named after the French town of Nîmes, where it was originally used to make sturdy work clothes. Today there's a denim trend to suit everyone. Whether it's classic blue jeans and a denim jacket, indigo skinnies, a flared skirt or even dungarees, no wonder fashion brands like Dsquared[2] and D&G do special denim-only collections.

Double denim or just a touch of blue: What's your denim look?

HELLO SAILOR

Cruise collections were originally created for rich fashion lovers who travelled to warm places in winter. These days, lots of fashion houses do cruise collections (sometimes known as holiday collections). A nautical theme – think Jean Paul Gaultier's sailor pants and stripy tops – is one of the most popular looks.

You're about to set sail. What will you wear for an adventure on the ocean waves?

Park Life

Just because you're taking your pooch for a walk doesn't mean you have to look like a dog's dinner. With fashion brands such as Stella McCartney, Lacoste and Juicy Couture doing funky sportswear – think cute tracksuits and trendy sneakers – looking good and staying fit is a walk in the park.

It's time for walkies. Think of a look that's sporty and stylish.

Pedal Power

Cycling's a great way to get around. Whether you're running errands or exploring a new town, the trick to looking good on a bike is to keep things comfy and cool. A cute romper suit and ballet pumps, or cut-offs and ankle boots, are perfect. And if your basket's full, a retro satchel is ideal for storing your purse and keys.

Where are you cycling today, and what are you going to wear?

The Swinging Sixties

The 1960s were a time of fashion revolution. In London girls wore knee-high boots and ultra-short mini dresses by designer Mary Quant, while in Paris André Courrèges experimented with Space Age accessories and geometric jewellery made from brightly coloured PVC. Even crash helmets got a futuristic makeover!

How would you accessorize your 60s-inspired outfit?

Easy Does It

With its draped dresses, high-waisted flares and strappy blouson tops, fashion in the 1970s was laid back. Accessories were popular too, so adding long beaded necklaces, jewelled bangles and floppy hats made for a vibe that was chilled out and carefree.

Trousers or dress? What mood are you in today?

FESTIVAL CHIC

At festivals, not only can you listen to great music and hang out with friends, you get to wear amazing outfits. Camping and muddy fields mean you need a versatile wardrobe, so while a pretty dress and sunglasses are a must, waterproof boots and a poncho might just come in handy too.

What would you pack in your festival bag?

Hidden Identities

500 years ago masquerade balls were flamboyant events where people wore elaborate masks to disguise their identities. Today, big fashion parties often have a masquerade theme such as 'Fairytale Ball' or 'Animal Magic', giving guests the perfect opportunity to wear spectacular gowns and imaginative masks decorated with ears, feathers and jewels.

What masquerade character would you be and what would you wear?